Extreme Sports

Kayaking

by Bill Lund

CAPSTONE PRESS

MANKATO, MINNESOTA

C A P S T O N E   P R E S S
818 North Willow Street • Mankato, MN 56001

Printed in the United States of America.

Library of Congress Cataloging-in-Publication Data
Lund, Bill, 1954-
    Kayaking/by Bill Lund
    p. cm. -- (Extreme sports)
    Includes bibliographical references and index.
    Summary: Describes the history, equipment, and contemporary practice
of kayaking.
    ISBN 1-56065-428-7
    1. Kayaking--Juvenile literature. [1. Kayaking.] I. Title. II. Series.
GV783.L76 1996
797.1'22--dc20

                                                    96-24723
                                                       CIP
                                                        AC

Photo credits
Kevin O'Brien, 8, 12, 17, 22-30, 34, 36. Unicorn/J.Bisley,
14; Robert W. Ginn, 11; Jean Higgins, 20; V.E. Horne,
32; Ronald E. Portis, 6; Chuck Schmeiser, 4; Sohm, 19;
Richard West, 38; International Stock/Eric Sanford, cover.

Table of Contents

Words in **boldface** type in the text are defined in the Glossary in the back of this book.

Chapter 1

Kayaking

Many people are drawn to the water. Many people live near the water. People love water's beauty and its power.

For centuries, people have tried different ways to get around in the water. Kayaking is one of the most basic ways. It is also a fun way.

A kayak is a narrow, lightweight boat. People have used kayaks in oceans and lakes. They have used kayaks in calm streams and rushing rivers.

The kayak was first used for basic transportation. Few people use a kayak for transportation anymore. Most people use kayaks for just plain fun.

Kayaking is a basic and fun way to get around in water.

Chapter 2

The Kayak

Modern kayaks are made of **fiberglass**. They can be from nine to 18 feet (about three to five meters) long.

The top of the kayak is called the deck. The hole in the deck is called the cockpit. The person navigating the kayak sits there.

Most kayaks are built with one cockpit. Some kayaks, though, are built with two cockpits. Two people can **navigate** these boats.

Kayaks are very buoyant. Buoyant means they float easily. A kayak will float even if it gets **swamped** with water.

Modern kayaks are made of fiberglass.

Kayaks use **polyethylene** foam to get their high buoyancy. Polyethylene is lighter than water. That is why it floats. Polyethylene is put in a kayak's **bow** and **stern**.

The Paddle

Kayakers move their boats with a paddle. Kayaking paddles are two-headed. Two-headed paddles have a flat blade on both ends. Paddles for most other boats have a flat blade only on one end.

Paddles are made of wood, fiberglass, aluminum, or other lightweight materials. The blades are nearly at **right angles** to each other. This helps the kayaker steer the boat. Kayakers want their paddles to be about an arm's length longer than their own height.

Canoes and Kayaks

Most people know what a canoe looks like. Canoes are more common than kayaks. Canoes and kayaks have some similarities.

Both are lightweight and long. Both are usually designed to hold just one or two

Kayakers use a two-headed paddle.

people. The skills you need to navigate a canoe and a kayak are very similar.

Canoes and kayaks have some differences, too. A canoe has an open top. Canoes can store camping gear that a kayak cannot.

A kayak has a covered top. It has polyethylene foam in its front and rear. It cannot carry much gear.

Portaging

Canoes are easy to carry, or **portage**. Canoes can be carried easily on two people's shoulders. A canoe can be used for shelter if it rains.

A kayak cannot be carried as easily. Kayaks do not make good shelters. A kayak is better than a canoe in rough waters, though. The kayak's high buoyancy makes it almost impossible to swamp.

A kayak can be steered more easily than a canoe. Kayakers always use a two-headed paddle. Canoeists almost always use a one-headed paddle.

A kayak is not easy to carry across land.

Chapter 3

History of the Kayak

Native Americans were living in North America thousands of years before the Europeans arrived. The Native Americans living in the cold Arctic regions of Canada and Alaska were called Eskimos.

Eskimos invented the kayak thousands of years ago. Early Eskimo kayaks were made of sealskin. They stretched the skin over a frame made of animal bones and wood. There are no trees where the Eskimos live.The wood had drifted in from the ocean.

Kayaks today are still based on early Eskimo designs.

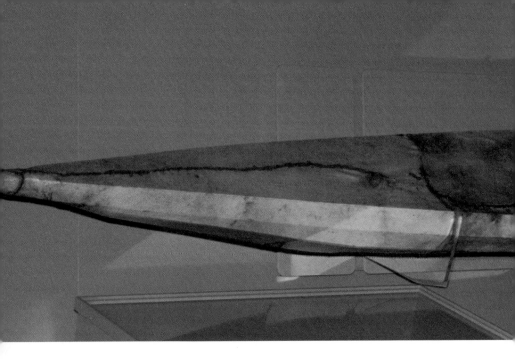

Using Animals

The Eskimos used animal **bladders** to make the kayaks buoyant. They took the bladders from animals they hunted. They hunted seals, polar bears and caribou. They filled the bladders with air before they put them underneath the sealskin.

The Eskimos tied their kayaks together with **sinews**. Sinews hook an animal's muscles to its bones. They are like strong, thick string. Eskimos used sinews from seals.

Eskimo kayaks were made from seal skins.

The Eskimos' kayaks were about 18 feet (5.4 meters) long. They were only two feet (60 centimeters) wide. They were lightweight. They moved fast in the water. They were perfect for hunting and fishing.

Most people today kneel in their kayaks. The Eskimos sat in their kayaks, though. They wore waterproof parkas. They fastened the parkas around the rim of the kayak's cockpit. This made the kayak watertight. It kept the Eskimo kayakers dry.

The Eskimo Roll

Eskimos used their kayaks in icy waters. If the boat **capsized**, the passengers could die in the cold water. To save themselves, they developed the Eskimo roll.

The Eskimo roll is a special move kayakers use if they tip over and are trapped upside down underwater. They use their paddles to flip the kayak upright. Kayakers today learn the Eskimo roll as a basic way to rescue themselves.

Kayaks in England

English explorers first saw Eskimos using kayaks in the 1500s. They saw them in the northern seas of North America. They took the idea back to Europe.

In 1865, an Englander named John MacGregor toured Europe in a kayak he built. He named the kayak *Rob Roy*. This was the first time people in Europe had seen a kayak.

Kayak students learn the Eskimo roll.

Later, MacGregor started the Royal Canoe Club of Great Britain. In England, kayaks were mistakenly called canoes. The Royal Canoe Club held the first organized kayak races in 1867.

Kayaks in Germany and the Olympics

The German people thought the kayak would be perfect for mountain rivers. They developed a **collapsible** kayak. It could be carried in bundles the size of two suitcases. People could take it to hard-to-reach places.

The kayak became popular around the world in the early part of the 20th century. Races were held both in calm rivers and in rapids called **wildwater**. Kayak racing became an Olympic event for the 1936 Summer Games held in Berlin, Germany.

Fiberglass Kayaks

Many new materials were invented for military use during World War II (1939-1945). Fiberglass was one of these materials. Fiberglass is strong and light.

Fiberglass kayaks are strong and inexpensive.

Fiberglass was first used to make kayaks in the 1950s. Fiberglass kayaks were much lighter. They were easier to take care of than the older boats. They were also less expensive. More people could afford to take part in the sport.

Chapter 4

Types of Kayaking

Kayaks are used in many different ways. Some people use kayaks to enjoy the peace and beauty of the great outdoors. Some people use kayaks because they enjoy the speed and competition. Others do wild stunts and tricks in their kayaks.

Calm-Water Kayaking

Most kayakers start with calm-water kayaking. Calm-water kayaking is done on fairly calm rivers, lakes, or ponds. Calm-water kayaking is done on inland bodies of water.

Some people use kayaks to enjoy the outdoors.

Inland bodies of water are not affected by ocean currents and waves.

Calm-water kayaking is a fun and relaxing way to enjoy the natural scenery. Kayakers who want more thrills practice paddling and **maneuvering** in calm water before they move on.

Wildwater Kayaking

Wildwater is river water that rushes fast around rocks and down falls. Wildwater is sometimes called whitewater. The water appears white when it splashes against the rocks.

Many kayakers like the thrill of maneuvering through rapids and wildwater. Some kayakers actually go over small waterfalls. Many kayakers ride through **canyons**. The water there moves especially fast because it is squeezed through these narrow spaces.

Wildwater kayakers need to learn many skills. They cannot let the water control the kayak. Instead, the water must flow around the

Many kayakers enjoy the thrill of wildwater.

sides of the kayak. That means the kayaker must steer carefully through the fast water.

Many kayakers enter wildwater competitions. These competitions are races. They are run on river courses. The courses are about two miles (about three kilometers) long.

The races may take up to 30 minutes. Competitors take off one at a time. They are timed. They try to pick the fastest way down the river. The racer with the quickest time wins.

Slalom

Slalom is another type of competition. Slalom events are usually held in wildwater. Slalom is the most popular form of kayak competition. The slalom tests how well people can maneuver their kayaks.

Slalom organizers set up 20 to 25 gates on a course. To make the gates, the organizers string rope above the river. The rope goes from one bank to the other.

The organizers hang two poles from the rope. The poles are far enough apart for a

Slalom kayakers steer through gates.

kayak to fit between them. The gate is the area
between the poles. The gates are numbered.
They are set so the kayakers have to zigzag
their way across the river.

Race Against Time

The competitors begin from the same starting line. They must maneuver their kayaks through the gates in order, beginning with gate one. Each competitor is timed.

Competitors cannot hit the poles when they go through the gates. If they do, five seconds are added to their score. If kayakers miss the gates completely, 50 seconds are added to their score.

The kayaker who finishes the course in the shortest amount of time wins.

A Popular Competition

The first kayak slalom was held in 1949. It took place in Switzerland. Since then, the slalom has grown popular worldwide.

Today, there is a world kayak slalom championship held every year. Kayakers from more than 25 countries compete in it.

The kayak slalom is particularly popular in England. In that country, there are more than

Slalom kayakers lose time when they hit poles.

5,000 people registered as competitive slalom kayakers.

Hot-dogging

Kayakers learned hot-dogging from skiers. They saw skiers jumping in the air, doing flips and midair splits. They watched them do stunts and tricks on the snow and in the water.

The skiers' tricks pleased the big crowds that gathered. The kayakers learned that the goal in hot-dogging is to do stunts that are original and exciting. They decided to develop hot-dog kayaking

Hot-dogging is almost always done in wildwater. Some hot-dog kayakers do somersaults with their kayaks. They throw their paddles in the air. They twirl their paddles like batons. Some balance their kayak on its bow for several seconds.

Hot-dogging is challenging. It is fun for participants and spectators. It has become popular quickly. The first World Stunt Boat Championships were held in 1991. Kayakers from five countries participated.

Hot-dog kayakers learned their tricks from skiers.

Squirt Boating

Some hot-doggers do stunts in squirt boats. Squirt boats are small kayaks. They are custom-made to fit each individual kayaker.

Because squirt boats are so small, they allow kayakers to do exciting tricks. Squirt boaters can do cartwheels. They can shoot through midair.

Squirt boating was first developed in the United States. It is always done in whitewater.

Kayak Polo

Kayak polo takes place in swimming pools instead of in rivers. Kayak polo players compete in teams of five. The goal is to toss the ball into the water polo net. They can use either the paddle or their hands.

Kayak polo is an exciting game. Safety is important. It is easy to hit a player with the ball or a paddle. Most players wear helmets and face guards. These protect them from getting injured.

Small stunt kayaks are called squirt boats.

Chapter 5
Safety First

The smartest kayakers think about safety before they get into a kayak. They want kayaking to be both fun and safe. They know they need the right skills and the right equipment.

Swimming and Paddling Skills

Kayakers will end up in the water, even if they are very skilled and very careful. That is why kayakers must know how to swim well.

Kayakers learn tricks to help them when they tip their boats over. The Eskimo roll is one of these tricks.

Smart kayakers learn how to be safe before they ever get into a kayak.

Experienced kayakers teach new kayakers special paddle strokes. These strokes help kayakers stay afloat in difficult situations.

Life Jackets

Kayaks stay afloat better than almost any other boat. But even the best kayakers are going to capsize sometimes. Then they need something to keep them afloat until help comes.

Life jackets keep the kayakers floating. Life jackets keep a kayaker's mouth and nose out of the water. That way they can breathe until help comes. Life jackets are especially helpful if a kayaker is knocked unconscious. Nothing is more important to kayakers than their life jackets.

Helmets

Many kayakers ride in wildwater. Others ride in the ocean surf. These kayakers should always wear helmets.

Kayak helmets are small and lightweight. They have hard plastic on the outside. The

Kayakers should wear hemets and life jackets.

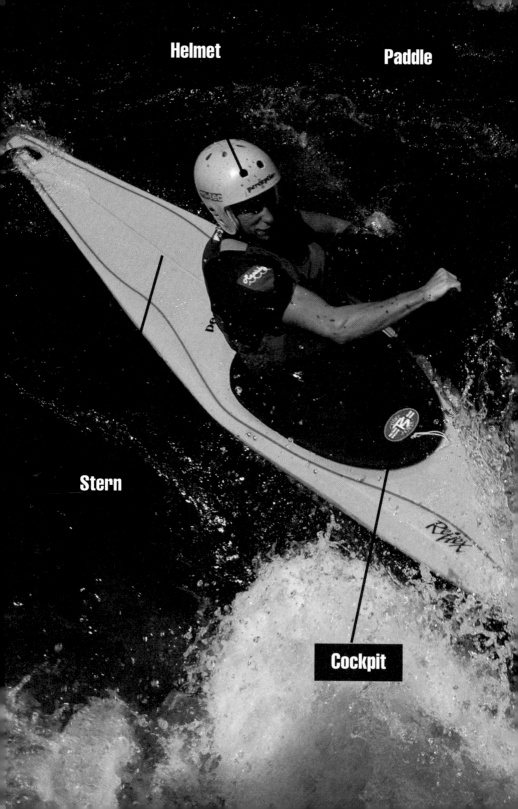

Helmet

Paddle

Stern

Cockpit

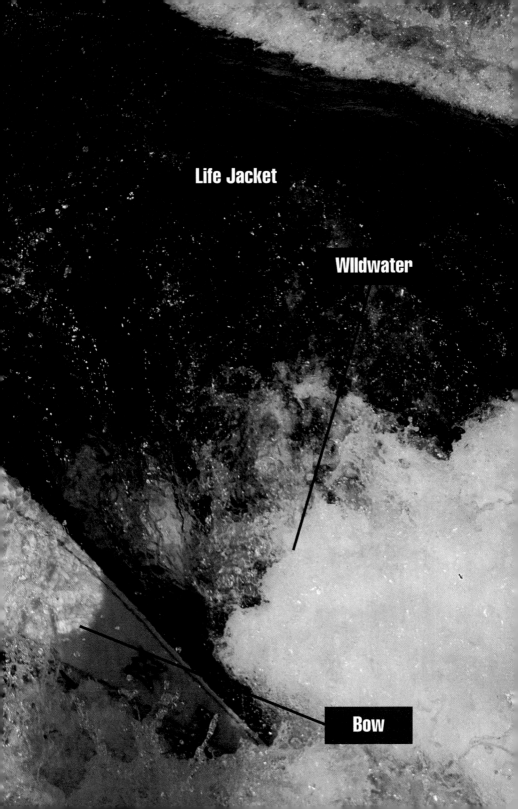

Life Jacket

Wildwater

Bow

inside is lined with foam. The helmet protects a kayaker if his or her head hits a rock or the kayak itself.

Fun for Everyone

Kayaking is not a popular form of general transportation, anymore. It is popular as a type of international competition, though. New forms of kayak competitions are being developed all the time.

There are more kayakers in the word than ever before. Most kayakers do not compete. They get into a kayak for simple reasons. They think kayaking is some of the best fun you can have in the water.

Kayaking can be fun for everyone.

The International Scale of River Difficulty

In general, rapids on a river fit into the following classifications. There are two conditions, however, that increase a river's difficulty. If the water temperature is below 50 degrees Fahrenheit (10 degrees Celsius), the river is considered one class more difficult than normal. Also, if the trip is an extended one in a wilderness area, the river is considered one class more difficult than normal.

Class I: Moving water with a few riffles and small waves; few or no obstructions.

Class II: Easy rapids with waves up to three feet (about one meter), and wide, clear channels that are obvious without scouting; some maneuvering is required.

Class III: Rapids with high, irregular waves often capable of swamping an open canoe;

narrow passages that often require complex maneuvering; may require scouting from shore.

Class IV: Long, difficult rapids with constricted passages that often require precise maneuvering in very turbulent waters; scouting from shore often necessary; rescue difficult; generally not possible for open canoes; boaters in covered canoes and kayaks should be able to Eskimo roll.

Class V: Extremely difficult, long and violent rapids with highly congested routes which nearly always must be scouted from shore; rescue conditions difficult; significant hazard to life in event of a mishap; ability to Eskimo roll essential.

Class VI: Difficulties of Class V carried to the extreme of navigability; nearly impossible and very dangerous; for teams of experts only, after close study and with all precautions taken.

The Eskimo Roll

Step one: The kayaker holds the paddle to the side as the kayak begins to go under.

Step two: While underwater, the kayaker pushes down on the paddle, turning the kayak.

Step three: The kayaker twists his or her body around while pushing on the paddle.

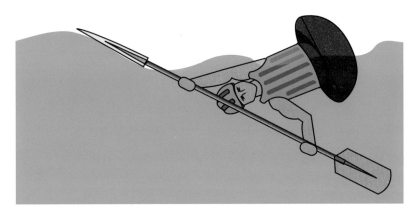

Step four: These combined motions roll the kayak all the way around, bringing the kayaker out of the water.

Glossary

bladder—a bag-like internal organ found in many animals; can be inflated with liquids or gases

bow—the front end of a boat

canyon—a narrow valley between high cliffs, often with a river flowing through it

capsize—when something gets overturned, especially a boat

collapsible—something that folds into itself, making it smaller for carrying

fiberglass—a plastic-like material made from glass fibers

maneuvering—moving something from one place to another in a controlled manner

navigate—to steer or direct something toward a specific place

polyethylene—a soft, moldable substance used to make a strong, clear, lightweight plastic

portage—to carry boats and supplies overland between waterways

right angle—an angle of 90 degrees
sinew—a tendon that connects muscle to bone
stern—the back end of a boat
swamp—to flood or sink a boat with water
wildwater—fast, rough water; sometimes called whitewater

To Learn More

Burch, David. *Fundamentals of Kayak Navigation.* Seattle: Pacific Search Press, 1987.

Evans, Eric and Jay Evans. *The Kayaking Book.* Lexington, Mass.: The Stephen Green Press, 1988.

Evans, Jeremy. *Whitewater Kayaking.* New York: Crestwood House, 1992.

Sanders, William. *Kayak Touring.* Harrisburg, Pa.: Stackpole Books, 1984.

Useful Addresses

American Canoe Association
P.O. Box 1190
Newington, VA 22122

American Whitewater Affiliation
6 Farnum St.
Cazenovia, NY 13035

Canadian Canoe Association
1600 James Naismith Drive
Gloucester, ON K1B 5N4
Canada

Canadian Whitewater Association
1283 Crescent Road
Surrey, BC V4A 2V6
Canada

National Association for River Sports
314 North 20th Street
Colorado Springs, CO 80904

Internet Sites

Being There
http://www.valpro.com/cgibin/var/valpro/
bethere/index.htm

Nick's Kayak Page
http://www.mindport.net/~schade/Kayak.html

Placid Videos
http://www.gorp.com/placid.htm

Saskatchewan Documented Canoe Routes
http://regina.ism.ca/trakker/outadv/canoe/
cdocumen.htm

Index